THE JUDGMENT OF THE LORD

THE FINAL WARNING

WRITTEN BY: LINDA K. WILLIES

ILLUSTRATIONS BY: LINDA K. WILLIES

The Seven Angels which had Seven Trumpets prepared themselves to sound; I heard a Great Voice out of the Temple, saying to the Seven Angels, go your Ways and Pour out the Vials of the Wrath of God upon the Earth. For thy Judgments are made manifest.

And I beheld, and heard Angel Flying through the Midst of Heaven saying with a Loud Voice, Woe, Woe, Woe, to the Inhabitants of the Earth

.

THE JUDGMENT OF THE LORD
THE FINAL WARNING
Illustrations by Linda K. Willies
ISBN: 13:9780999777671
ISBN:10:099977767X

The prophetic words and illustrations in this book are those
of the Holy Spirit given to the author.
All scriptures are taken from (KJV) Bible

Published by
B-Inspired Publishing
7285 Winchester Road, Suite 109
Memphis, TN 38125
www.B-Inspiredpub.com
Printed in the United States
First Edition: January 2019

Book design and Interior design copyright @2019 by
B-Inspired Publishing, LLC.

Religion/Biblical Studies/Prophecy

TABLE OF CONTENTS

SAYS THE LORD--*1*

PREFACE--*2*

ACKNOWLEDGMENT--*3*

INTRODUCTION---4

   I AM THAT I AM--*4*

CHAPTER 1--10

   GOD THE FATHER JUDGMENT-------------------------------------*10*

   UPON THE EARTH--*10*

CHAPTER 2--14

   GOD THE SON NOW IS THE JUDGMENT OF THIS WORLD--------*14*

CHAPTER 3--18

   THE AFFIRMATION OF THE FINAL WARNING------------------------*18*

CHAPTER 4---19

   THE SPIRIT OF HOLINESS---*19*

CHAPTER 5---21

   GOD THE HOLY SPIRIT THE FINAL WARNING---------------------------*21*

CHAPTER 6---25

   AMERICA'S CALAMITIES---*35*

DESOLATION---39

CATASTROPHE--39

CHAPTER 7---40

   A PRAYER OF REPENTANCE UNTO SALVATION-----------------------*41*

CHAPTER 8 SAYS THE LORD GOD--------------------44

CHAPTER 9 THE FINAL WARNING------------------46

   TO A REBELLIOUS PEOPLE---*46*

THE JUDGMENT OF THE LORD ----------------------49

THE FINAL WARNING--46

SAYS THE LORD

Consider what I say; for the Lord gives you understanding

In all things, in that of:

The Anti-Christ is in the Earth

The Mark of the Beast is in the Earth

The False Prophet is in the Earth

Perilous Times shall remain in the Earth

The Holy Spirit is in the Earth

The Final Warning is in the Earth

II Timothy 2:7

PREFACE

In the days of the Voice of the Seventh Angel, when he shall begin to Sound, the Mystery of God should be finished, as declared to his Servants the Prophets. Which Heaven must receive until the Times of Restitution of all things, which God has spoken by the mouth of all his Holy Prophets since the World began.

A noise shall come even to the Ends of the Earth: for the Lord has a controversy with the Nations, He will give them that are wicked to the Sword. The Lords appointed Time of his Prophecies is aligned on His Timetable for Humanity whose Time has come. He shall send forth the prophets to declare it, manifesting His purpose in the Earth. Judgment originates from God and the prophet proclaims it.

The Lord God gives and releases His Word to the Prophets to bear and carry in the Earth until His purpose is fulfilled.

2

When the Prophets of God prophesy the Lords Judgment, then the Angelic Angels of the Most High God are released to enforce it, executing His Judgments in the Earth.

Time Is of a Lesser, and Days of an Ending

ACKNOWLEDGMENT

I give all the Honor and Glory to my beloved Lord and Savior, Christ Jesus my Redeemer. I thank the Lord, who privileged me, His Daughter of Zion, in that He counted me worthy to receive and declare The Judgment of the Lord, the Final Warning unto the Nations.

Who is he to whom the mouth of the Lord has spoken, that he may declare it?

In the early morning hours around three O'clock, January 1st of 1995, the Holy Spirit awaken me to write His Words of Judgment the Final Warning. Son of Man, I have made you a Watchman unto the House of Zion: therefore hear the Word of My Mouth, and give them Warning from me. While I was writing the Lords message, my soul was shaken to such Reverential Fear for which I had never known before in Christ Jesus, God the Righteous Judge. He

4

instructed and charged unto me, do not reveal or speak it to anyone for it is not time.

This book was written in completion by the inspiration of the Holy Spirit and of the Doctrine of Christ: in March of 2018. This is the Generation for whom in which the Lord of Host, the God of Glory has pronounced this Judgment: He shall call to the Heavens from above, and to the Earth, that He may Judge humanity. This Word which came down from Heaven is written in the Earth to be His Final Word and Warning as of the Prophecies in the Book of Revelation. All that I have acknowledged is Said and true of my Lord and Savior who gave to me to write; His True Sayings, for the Witness of God is Greater than the witness of man. If any man speaks, let him speak as the Oracles of God; that God the Father in all things may be glorified through Christ Jesus. To whom be the Praise and the Glory and Dominion from Everlasting to Everlasting. Lord I thank you, because you have hidden these things from the wise and prudent and

have revealed them unto whosoever thy will.

Ezek 3:17; Jer 9:12; Jeremiah 50:4; 1Pt 4:11; Matt11:25

INTRODUCTION

ש לכך
I AM THAT I AM

S ays the Lord God, He that Created the Heavens, and stretched them out; I have made the Earth, and Created man upon it. I AM, He that spread forth the Earth, and that which comes forth out of it; I AM, He that gives breath unto the people upon it, and Spirit to them that walk therein. I AM, the True Living God; in my Wrath, the Earth shall tremble, and the Nations shall not be able to abide my Indignation.

Behold, I will cause to cease out of this place (Earth) in your eyes, and in your days, the voice of laughter, the voice of gladness, the voice of the grooms' and their brides'. For many walks after the flesh, whose end is destruction, whose god is their belly, and whose glory is in their shame, who mind earthly things.

They shall say for what reason has the Lord pronounced all

of His Judgments against us? What is our Iniquity? What is our Sin which we have committed against the Lord God Elohim? Says the Lord, for mine eyes are upon all their ways: They are not hidden from my face, neither is their iniquity hid from mine eyes. Yes, the stork in the heaven knows her appointed times; and the turtle and the crane and the swallow observe the time of their coming, but the man knows not the Judgment of the Lord. They are foolish, for they know not the way of the Lord, nor the Judgment of the True Living God.

The earth shall be desolate because of them that dwell therein, for the fruit of their deeds. I AM, the Righteous Judge, He who comes to Judge, with Righteousness shall I Judge the World and all Humanity. Behold, all the inhabitants shall know My Mighty Hand; and they shall know that my Name is The Lord. I AM, that I AM, the Lord God, who has declared His Judgment for the

Generation of the End Times; the Generation of Wrath.

I AM GOD, and there is none like me, declaring the End from the Beginning and from Ancient Times the things that are not yet done. I AM the Lord; and there is none else.

I AM, Alpha and Omega, the Beginning and the Ending.

Reference: Isa 42:5; Jer 10:10; 8:7; 16:9, 21; Phil 3:19; II Tim 4:16, 17; Matt 10:10; 16:10, 17; Micah 7:13, Isa 45:18; 46:9, 10; Rev 21:16

CHAPTER 1

אלוהימהאב
GOD THE FATHER
JUDGMENT UPON THE EARTH

" **S** ays the Lord, Heaven is my Throne, and the Earth is my Footstool." The Lord looked down from Heaven upon the children of men, to see if there were any that did understand, and seek God.

They are not valiant for the Truth upon the Earth; for they proceed from evil to evil, and they know Me not, says the Lord. For a voice of wailing is heard out of Zion, how are we ruined! We are greatly confounded, because we have forsaken the Earth, because of our iniquities and transgressions.

This is a nation (Zion) that obeyed not the voice of the Lord their God, nor received correction in Truth: for Truth is

10

perished and is cut off from their mouths. I AM, the Lord which exercise Loving Kindness, Judgment, and Righteousness in the Earth: for in these things I delight, says the Lord.

I AM the hope of Zion, all them that forsake me shall be ashamed, and they that depart from me shall be written in the "Earth", because they have forsaken the Lord, the Fountain of Living Waters.

Behold, the days come, says the Lord, that I will punish all them which are circumcised with the uncircumcised. The Lord shall call to the Havens from above, and to the Earth, that He may Judge humanity.

This matter is of Decree of the Angels and the command by the Word of the Holy Ones: to the intent that the living may know that the most High God rules in the Kingdom of man, and gives it to whomsoever He will, and appoint over it, men that are prudent in speech. He will do according to his will among the inhabitants in the Earth: and no man can stop or say, what does thou doeth?

The whole Earth was of one language, and of one speech. And the Lord came down to see the city and the tower, which the children of men built. Come, let us go down and there confound their language that they may not understand one another's speech. So the Lord scattered them abroad from there, upon the face of all the earth: and they left off from building the tower. Therefore is the name of it called Babel; because the Lord did there confound the language of all the Earth: and from there did the Lord scatter them abroad upon the face of all the Earth.

God shall bring every work into judgment with every secret thing, whether it is good, or whether it is evil. Behold, the whirlwind of the Lord goes forth with wrath, a continuing whirlwind: I will fan them with a Wind that blows in the Gates of the Earth. The fierce anger of the Lord shall not return until He has performed the intents of His Heart.

Arise, O God, Judge the Earth: for you shall inherit all Nations. Hear O' Earth and all you people that dwell therein; the Lord God cometh from His Holy place, of witness against you. Behold; the Lord God cometh and will come down upon all, the inhabitants that dwells in the earth.

Reference: Jer 9:3,19,24 ,25 7:28; Dan 4:17,35; Gen 11:1,5,7,8; Eccl 12:14,13,7 Jer 17:13; 30:23,24; Ps 14:2; 82:8; Micah 1:2

CHAPTER 2

בןאלוהים
GOD THE SON
NOW IS THE JUDGMENT
OF THIS WORLD

He that cometh from above is above all: I heard a Loud Voice saying in Heaven, now is come Salvation and Strength, and the Kingdom of our God, and the Power of His Christ. He shall not fail nor be discouraged, until He has set Judgment in the Earth. In the beginning was the Word, and the Word was God, the same was in the beginning with God. And the Word was made flesh, and dwelt among us, and we beheld His Glory, the Glory as of the only begotten of the Father, full of Grace and Truth. Which was born, not of blood, nor of the will of the flesh, nor of the will of man, but of God. This is the

Condemnation, that Light comes into the World; men loved darkness rather than Light, because their works are evil.

I come, A Light into the World, I came forth from the Father, and I come into the World. The Son of Man came not to be ministered unto but to Minister, and to give His Life a Ransom for many. Think not that I am come to send peace on Earth; I came not to send Peace, but a Sword. The Father who sent Me, He gave Me a Commandment what I should say and what I should speak. I will declare the decree: the Lord has said unto Me, I spoke openly to the World; I ever taught in the Synagogue and in the Sanctuary and in secret have I hid nothing.

To this end was I born, and for this cause I came into the World, that I, should bear witness unto the Truth; every one that is of the Truth hears my Voice. I came forth from the Father, and I come into the World; the World cannot hate you; but Me it hates, because I testify of it. **That the**

Works there in are Evil, for Judgment I come into this World. You are from beneath, I am from above: you are of this World; I am not of this World. **I came down from Heaven, not to do My Own Will, but the Will of Him that Sent Me.** "If I had not come and spoken unto them (In the Earth), and they had not had sin: **but now, they have no excuse for their Sin, for there is no more of a Sacrifice."**

Father, I have Glorified you in the Earth; I have finished the Work you gave Me to do, that the World may believe that you sent Me. I depart and leave the World, and return to the Father, My Kingdom is not of this World. I was believed on in the World, Manifest in the Flesh, seen of Angels, justified in the Spirit, and Preached unto the Gentiles. I AM, Glory, Seated on the Right Hand of God the Father, the Scepter of Righteousness. I AM, King of Kings and Lord of Lords, "for the Father Judges no man, but has committed all Judgment unto the Son, and has given all

Authority to execute Judgment. "I AM thy Righteous Judge".

Reference: Matt 10:34; 18:11; 20:28; Mk 10:14; Jn1:1-14; 7:7; 12:49, 14:11; 1Tim 3:16; Jn 3:19, 31; 6:38; 12:46; 17:21 18:37; 15:22Jn 16:28; 5:22; 27; Rev 1:18

CHAPTER 3

THE AFFIRMATION OF
THE FINAL WARNING

These sayings Are Faithful and True: He that is unjust, let him be unjust still And He which is **filthy**, let him be filthy still And He that is **righteous**, let him be righteous still And He that is **holy**, let him be holy still To whom shall I speak, and give warning, that they may hear. Hear all nations, all people, come and hear; let the earth hear and all that dwells therein. The world and all things that come forth of it. **For the indignation of the Lord is upon all Nations.**

Reference: Rev 22:6, 11; Jer 6:10; Isa 34:1, 2

CHAPTER 4

THE SPIRIT OF HOLINESS

When the (Holy Spirit), Spirit of Righteousness comes, He will reprove the World of Sin, of Righteousness and of Judgment, because the prince of this World is Judged. The Holy Spirit whom the Father will send in my name, He shall teach you all things.

"Whosoever speaks a Word against the Holy Spirit, it shall not be forgiven by him, neither in this World, and neither in the World to come."

O' Faithless and perverse generation, how long shall I be with you? How long shall I suffer with you? From the Time of Pentecost until now; I am in long-suffering of completion, upon Redeeming the Souls of men, unto Righteousness. To receive Salvation in Christ Jesus, God the Eternal Glory.

Reference: Jn 16:8, 11; Matt 12:32, 17:17;

CHAPTER 5

אלוהים את רוח הקודש
GOD THE HOLY SPIRIT
THE FINAL WARNING

They are not all in my perfect will, all those who say they are of me, even those who go to church and take communion and praise me with their mouths. I shall return for a Holy People and I shall not repent on this saying. They that say I AM of no importance, in doing all of the things that they do to please their flesh, and not care of what they will be or become.

I AM, not pleased with these that says I am a Christian and a person who is not going around doing bad things. But these are they that are a bad bunch of nothing. Because they serve me not, nor care to be of a Holy Living in me. They will not be with me when I come, because they chose to live

21

as they want. This is not a reason for them to change, they will only change, if I change or if I call out war upon the land or if I appear in a moment and take up those who did my will. Soon I shall change the things that are making all who say that they are of me. They who do all as the sinners shall not be with me in my house.

These things are of a True Saying, if anyone does not believe these sayings are truly blind and on their way to destruction. They are not aware of who has them blinded; they only know that they are in a world of pleasures. All who do not think on me at all shall not live long. I AM, of a Higher Level and can see all that they do. No one can hide anything from me. These days are of a Last Generation, who will not be in my House. Soon, I will sort the Sheep from the Goat, and I will not allow any of my Sheep be mixed with the Goats, for they are Sanctified and Holy unto me. All they that love this world shall not live with God the

Father and God the Son and God the Holy Spirit.

I AM, at a place where all who know me, for they are aware of these that live on this place called Earth. **I AM Eternal and I AM, Eternity**, for they know not what these here do, they only live of Joy and Peace and they live unto seeing the Lord when He comes. They are in my place where they know not of the things that take place in this earthly realm.

This is a True Saying, those who do not believe shall be lost, and they shall never see my face or of my place. I AM, of a Higher Realm, they that are of me are of my Spirit and shall see me when I come. **All who know not of me will not be able to live any time after I have come and taken my people away with me.** Soon, all will not use their days as though they have a long life to live in pleasures. Soon, those who do not know who I AM, will know me after everyone has left this place and who does not want to be destroyed in a place where there is nothing but death. Those who do not know me will say all of this is not true, shall not receive any of my blessings. I AM, of all them that Loves Me and I will not leave them nor forsake them. Those who say, I AM, something that is of a natural source shall not live as those who live in me. I AM, all and of all those who are in me as a flower that will not need to be watered as if it is needed on a daily basis. When I come, they shall know that I AM, already in a perpetual state and I shall not leave any of my flowers un-watered and they shall be uprooted and wrapped in me. This is a True Saying; all who do not hear my voice will not be saved. I shall appear when the times are fulfilled, and my Father has sent me to gather all of His Children, who loves Him. This is not all of them whom I will be in when a Sound comes from the Wind. I will be in them that is a Holy Vessel and that is of my Spirit. They will not receive the thing that is of the System of this World.

This is a true saying and I have spoken in My Truth, and I have declared all that I say to be decreed as My Final Word on each matter in reference to the things I 'am performing in the coming days that is of a sign to them who believes in me. Many shall say this is not a Truth and it is a Lie, and all those who say these things shall not be with me in my Kingdom. This is a Truth that cannot be mentioned in a mouth that has no Life or Partaking of Me. I AM, not a source who is of a thing or an obvious thing that cannot be used or cannot be seen. They think, I AM, of something that has no life or that is of no substance in this World. All who say I AM, not real shall know of me from the Pit once they enter in. This is a truth and it shall stand and shall not be altered or changed, because it is My Word that comes from my Mouth. All those who are of me will not always be in a place of mourning but shall be of a place of rejoicing. This is all and all of My Truth and it shall not be alter nor added, for I AM, He who has spoken and has given to my Anointed to write to those who do not know me.

All who hear and who understand, shall not be forgiven if they choose not to turn from their ungodly living in which I have no part in their doing. This is a Truth and is My Word, Now and Forever and Ever. This is my Final Word and Warning to all who do not obey and who do not observe My Word in these True Sayings, as it is written of the word God, in the Doctrine of Christ.

When all who claim to be of me and are not of me shall be exposed and shall not know how it was found out about them. All who does not obey my true sayings shall be an enemy and a foe of mine. When they are in my presence they shall not be able to stand or be able to sit or be able to pray or be able to look or be able to last during my Words of Saying. All who say I AM not real shall not be among them that has a place in My Kingdom. This is a True Saying; this is My Word that is of Me and not of any man who has not My Spirit. This is a record that is of my bearing Witness with my Spirit and my Anointed Man of God. "All who say this is not true and is not of the Word of God shall be Chasten and shall be without my Blessings or my Anointing or my Spirit or my Love."

When a person who does all that they want to do and continue in doing the things as the World and yet calls upon Me for a Blessing and a Miracle, shall not receive a word in response to their prayers, because you, **"Praise Me with your lips and live unto the enemy"**, now you shall know that I AM, is not a rewarder to them that lives as my enemy. Soon, all shall know who I AM, and who I am coming for when the Times are fulfilled and when all my outpouring is over. Then shall they who did not receive My Spirit shall know that the Time is of a lesser and of a Final Ending for them who choose not to allow me to be Lord of their life, and of their living. Soon, these things shall all come to pass without any turning about or any reason for me to relinquish my Judgment and my Purpose of the Prophecy as in My Words of Old. All who do not understand shall want Me to save them from the things to come but it shall be too late, yes, it shall be too late. These are the True Sayings of God. All who do not believe my sayings shall be a byword and a token of my purpose for not obeying, when they call upon Me for their loss of my blessings. All those who are not of me shall be in a state of not knowing who or what is happening when I come for my people, who did do the things I have told them to do and who has not turned away from doing my works. All who say they know Me, but did not do anything, only lived day by day and did not think on Me, as to how or why, or should they partake in doing My Work. They shall be given a portion with them who did not know Me and who cared not for Me. These shall be taken and put in a bottle and shall be shaken as saline without flavor.

This is a True Saying, which comes from My Mouth and not of any man, says the Lord. Anyone who does not believe My Words shall not be with Me when I return for the Redeemed who obeyed and who continued in My Word. These things shall come to pass and they shall be a Sign to those who did do the things that I have commanded them to do." For all who does not believe My Words as I have spoken, My True Sayings as though it meant nothing, shall know My Wrath for not obeying. When all, the redeemed have left those behind and are rejoicing in My Presence, then those who were not invited shall weep and mourn for sorrow of heart and sorrow of regret and sorrow of repentance. This is a True Saying and is a True Record of My Word and of My Spirit and My Anointed Man of God. **If anyone does not believe My True Sayings because of a**

hardening of heart and of a rebellion against My Word shall not receive Eternal Life.

They will not know what Hour or what Time or what Day or the Year of when I shall appear. Only My Father and I know this event of the fullness of times. This a True Saying and a True Meaning and a True Witness of My Word and My Spirit and My Anointed Man of God. Soon, all will know this is a True Saying. This I commanded you, Obey my voice, and I will be your God, and you shall be my people; and that you walk in all the ways that I have commanded you that it may be well unto you. **"This is a True Saying and is My Word that comes forth out of My Mouth and shall not be changed; nor alter, nor added, nor deleted and this is my Final Warning concerning all who will not obey My Word, shall have a Just Recompense of My Judgment against them."**

This Earth cannot stand and cannot endure much longer in

standing and enduring the evil that is within itself. It will not last much longer because all of My Statues are not observed nor are performed nor thought of, because you did not want Me, nor will thyself to do as I have spoken, that is written of the Doctrine of Christ. These are my Words of Warning to all who know and did not do, as I have spoken in My Word. **They shall receive a Judgment and a Woe unto them for not obeying My Words of the Doctrine of Christ.**

Soon, all shall know who I AM, and who I am coming for, and who I will receive as My Own; and all others shall be my enemy. This is a True Saying and shall not be changed nor shall be altered nor shall be added nor shall be deleted. This is My Word that goes forth out of My Mouth and it shall stand in All Truth as I have spoken in the Name, of God the Father and God the Son and God the Holy Spirit. All who are not of Me shall be of a Great Trouble and shall not know where to run or where to hide. They shall be as one who is in a state of panic and a state of blind and a state of sorrow. They shall not be able to escape nor be able to hide. All who are not taken up shall be as these and shall weep and shall fast and shall seek Me. They shall not be heard, nor will I look upon them in My Mercy, they shall have what they just deserve. These are My True Sayings, My Truth which goes forth out of My Mouth and Declared of My Written Word. If anyone does not believe My Sayings, shall not be with Me nor shall I exclude them from these things to come. This is My Final Word and My Final Warning to all who do not obey as I have spoken. This is of Me and not of a man; this is of God the Father and God the Son and God the Holy Spirit.

These Judgments shall be to all of them and to all of the ones that have known My Words. These Judgments are of a space and of a time that shall be for all of those who did not look unto Me and unto My True Sayings. This shall be all and all in a space of three years and shall not be changed nor shorten because you did not Love the Lord thy God, as it was told to you in My Covenant. Now all shall be as I have spoken and as I have told you. All of My Truth shall come to pass and I shall perform all that I have spoken. This is a Truth, which goes forth out of My Mouth and not of any man. If anyone does not obey, shall not be with Me in My Kingdom nor shall I receive them when I come. This is all of Me and not of any man. This is My Word that goes forth out of My Mouth. My Word is that of God the Father and God the Son and God the Holy Spirit.

Humanity knows not what I do and they do not understand the things which happen in this earthly realm. These things that they see and hear are not all that will happen when I come. When I come, people will not know how I came into this earthly realm and did not leave My Chosen, the

Redeemed in a World that is full of Evil and Violence. These things will be in a space of three years and will be all that I have spoken in My Word. **When I have taken the Redeemed and the Innocent away and they are in My Eternity then will those who are left behind will cry out to me, and only then will they know that I AM REAL.**

This is all of My Truth, says the Lord, and not of any man. This is of God the Father and God the Son and God the Holy Spirit. This is My Final Word and My Final Warning to all of Humanity that dwells here in this Earthly Realm; for these Words are Faithful and True. These are the True sayings of God. *Rev 19:9* (This is the Word that the Lord had given me) (On January 1st 1995, Early Morning, 3: am the Holy Spirit awakens me and gives unto me to write. I was told to conceal and tell no one, for it is not time. In this I declare; my faith does not stand in the wisdom of men but in the Power of God, the Great I AM.)

CHAPTER 6

AMERICA'S CALAMITIES

I AM that I AM having heard the pride of America (she is exceeding proud) her loftiness, and her arrogance and her pride and the haughtiness of her heart.

<u>"America Woe unto thee"</u>; **behold, the Lord rides upon a Swift Cloud, releasing His Judgment unto a Nation**: I will set America against itself: and they shall fight every one against his Neighbor, City against City, and State against State. Where are the Wise men? Where are they? Let them tell you now, and let them know what the Lord of Hosts has purposed upon this Nation. Because you have trusted in thy works and in thy treasures, **thou shall also be taken.**

Says the Lord of Hosts; the God of Zion: Behold, I Will bring upon this Nation and upon all her Cities all the Evil

35

that I have Pronounced against it, because they have hardened their necks, that they might not obey My Words.

The calamity of America is near to come, and her afflictions hasten fast.

At this time shall it be said to this People; to America, "A Dry Wind of the High Places": in the Wilderness toward these people who are ungodly, not to Fan or to Cleanse. In that Day shall America be like Women: and they shall be afraid and fear because of the Shaking of the Hand of the Lord of Hosts, which He has released upon them. <u>To the Four Elements; hear and obey; O' Earth, Open up and Swallow, Mountains throw forth thy Fire, Dry Wind, Full Wind and Whirlwind Blow Down Fiercely, Waters of Oceans, Rage and Overflow</u>.

This shall be a Sign unto you from the Lord that the Lord will do this thing that He has Spoken: for Morning by Morning shall it Come, by Day and by Night shall it come:

then He shall make you understand, I AM the Potter and you are the Clay. You shall be judged of the Lord of Hosts with Great Storms, with Great Floods, and Burning Fire.

"Shout against her round about: she has given her hand: the <u>Foundations of (Righteousness)</u> are no more, <u>her walls (Precepts of God) are thrown down</u>; for Now is the Vengeance of the Lord. There shall be no more praise of America.

Take Vengeance upon her; as she has done, requite unto her the judgments of the Lord. Says the Lord, why cry for your afflictions? Your sorrow is incurable for the multitude of your iniquities: for your sins were increased. I have done these things unto you. The Lord have opened His Armory and have brought forth the Weapons of His Indignation: for this is the work of the Lord God of Hosts in the Land of America.

God the Creator of the Heavens and of the Earth will

give sentence against sin, commanding his Angelic Angels to carry out his Judgments upon the inhabitants in the Earth, out of its four kinds: Wind, Water, Earth, and Fire. God the Creator has given man the intelligence to understand their natural habitat of Seasons, Cycles and Patterns, yet man relies upon themselves as to think as themselves with instruments and tools predicting Atmospheric Weather conditions which effects the environments in which we live. Man and much of humanity whereas being ignorant of God's Spiritual Laws of Judgment against "Sin" that brings in destruction. **"For Her Transgressions are many and her Abominations are Great."** America has forgotten it is God the Creator who governs all Elements and Events.

Reference: Isa 19:1, 2, 16; 28:19; 29:6; 38:7; Jer 50:15; 15:6; 30:15; 48:2,7,16,29; 50:25

Given by the Holy Spirit on: 6/28/2013

DESOLATION

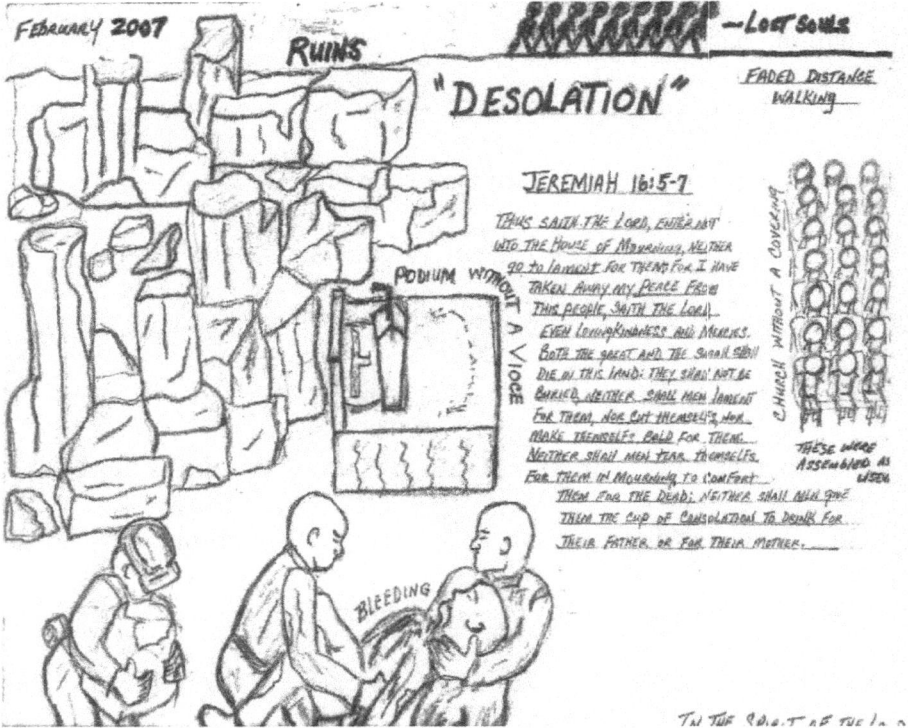

Prophetic Drawing year 2007

CATASTROPHE

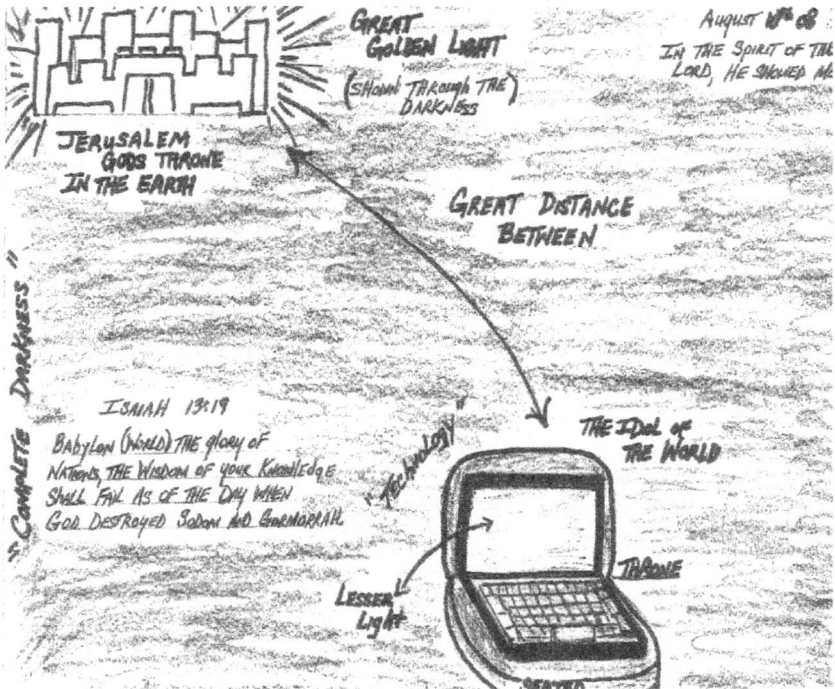

Prophetic Drawing year 2008

CHAPTER 7

A PRAYER OF REPENTANCE UNTO SALVATION

"I have not come to call the righteous but sinners to Repentance. "That whosoever believes in Him shall not perish but have Eternal Life. For God so Loved the World that He gave His only begotten Son, that whosoever believes in Him shall not perish, but have Everlasting Life.

In the name of Jesus:

Lord, I repent with a sincere heart of all my Sins, which I have committed. Lord your Word declares, if I confess with my mouth the Lord Jesus Christ, the Son of The True Living God, who died on the Cross and Shed His Precious Blood for me; whom you raised from the Dead, that whosoever believes on Him shall be Saved.

Heavenly Father, in the name of Jesus, **I believe in my Heart and confess with my mouth, my belief and confession of Faith in Jesus Christ is made unto Salvation**. For I believe in this truth, that the Son of God, Jesus Christ, came and Died on the Cross for my Sins; I believe that He Rose from the Dead and is the Resurrection. I believe that He is the Scepter of Righteousness; I believe that the Blood of Jesus washes away all my sins. I believe that I am, now redeemed from destruction.

Lord, I Thank You, that my Sins are forgiven by the Shed Blood of my Savior Jesus Christ, and that my name is written in the Lambs Book of Life. Lord, I Thank You which you have heard my confession of Faith unto Salvation in your Love for me; to the saving of My Soul unto Life Everlasting. Lord, I Thank You, that Jesus Christ the Son of the True Living God, is now the Lord of My Life. Amen, Amen and Amen.

Reference: Jn 3:15, 16; Rom 9:9, 10

CHAPTER 8

SAYS THE LORD GOD

The things that have come and things that are made and the things that shall be that has been Prophesied; these things will take place and they shall remind those who have read and known of all the Prophecies that are written. Many people will not be caught up with Me to depart from this Earthly Realm, and they shall Cry and Weep and Pray and Fast and they shall regret. All who continue to live in Sin and continue to deny Christ and Righteousness shall be as one who cannot see; spiritually blind. **All those who love their flesh shall never come into my Presence and know of my Holy Kingdom and my Love**.

Therefore, I will make the ungodly as a heap of the field as dung. And I will throw down the strong into the valley and all their Idols shall be crushed to powder. All the ungodly

44

shall be cast into the Fire with their Idols. **They believed Babylon the Harlot (Worldly System), and they shall return unto whom they believed.**

Given by the Holy Spirit on: 1-8-2004

CHAPTER 9

THE FINAL WARNING
TO A REBELLIOUS PEOPLE

Woe to a rebellious people, says the Lord, that take counsel, but not of Me. That cover with a covering, but not of My Spirit, that they may add sin to sin. All you Inhabitants of the World, and dwellers on the Earth, you shall see, when He; The Lord of Host, The God of Glory has performed His word before your eyes, **Signs of the End Times.**

Says the Lord, shall evil be recompensed for good?

These evil people, who refuse to hear my Words, which walk in the imagination of their heart, and walk after other gods (**Idols; Statues** and **Man**) to serve them and to worship them, shall know my wrath. Is it not for you to know my Judgment? Who hate the good and love the evil.

46

Woe unto them that call evil good, and good evil; that put darkness for light, and light for darkness; that put bitter for sweet, and sweet for bitter! For the Lord of Host shall be exalted in Judgment, and God who is Holy shall be Sanctified in Righteousness. The Lord lives, in Truth, in Judgment, and in Righteousness. I the Lord search the heart; I try the reins, even to give every man according to his ways and according to the fruit of his deeds. The Lord knows how to deliver the godly out of

Temptations, and to reserve the unjust unto the Day of Judgment to be punished.

The beginning of Wisdom is the "Fear" of the Lord!

Reference: Isa: 5:16, 20; 18:3; 30:1; 38:7; Jer 13:10; 4:2; 17:10; Micah 3:2; II Pt 2:9

THE JUDGEMENT OF THE LORD
THE FINAL WARNING

The Lord God gives and releases His Word to the Prophets to bear and carry in the Earth until His purpose is fulfilled. When the Prophets of God prophesy the Lords Judgment, then the Angelic Angels of the Most High God are released to enforce it, executing His Judgments in the Earth.
Time Is of a Lesser, and Days of an Ending.

About the Author

Linda, whose background of Christianity and Faith in Christ Jesus was from early childhood. Linda was always amazed and intrigued about cycles of life and seasonal changes of winter, spring, summer and autumn. To better understand life and its cycles, it would have to come from God the creator. Truth can only be revealed from the source of the creator as to why things are as they are. Her discipleship in Christ transformed from Baptist to Pentecostal into the teachings of the Kingdom of God. She was called and anointed into Prophetic Ministry of Christ Jesus as a Prophetic Writer. Linda's spiritual experiences and Prophetic Visions of the Lord accompany with his word, were given to be shared with believers alike and non-believers of a witness to the truth.

www.ingramcontent.com/pod-product-compliance
Lightning Source LLC
Chambersburg PA
CBHW022342040426
42449CB00006B/678